*For my mother - who she is and who she used
to be*

*For my children - who they are and who they
choose to be*

Presentation by *BookLeaf Publishing*

Web: www.bookleafpub.com

E-mail: info@bookleafpub.com

ISBN: 9789360941031

First edition 2024

Finding Equanimity

Michele Dubrouillet

PREFACE

Our lives were turned upside down when my mother was in a car accident in 2019. We had noticed strange behaviors in her before, but this was unprecedented. Afterwards, she couldn't remember the accident, and the hospital staff blamed her forgetfulness on her hitting her head and alcohol. Several days later she still was fuzzy on the details, and they gave her a test which showed some mental deficiency. Thus began a five year plus struggle to find out what was wrong and deal with that struggle amid the worry and fear. Still, beauty and joy bloom with us and around us every day.

The Phone Call

An English proverb once said,
"March comes in like a lion and goes out like a
lamb"
Unless
You get a call from paramedics
Telling you your mother has been in a car
accident
She should be okay, they say calmly
While you grab your bag and keys
So many thoughts invade your mind
Was she driving recklessly?
Did she get lost?
Thank goodness I'm off this week
What went wrong?
What. Went. Wrong?

The Diagnoses

The confusion is palpable.
Repeatedly, she asks what happened.
They tell her she was in a car accident.
Minutes pass and she asks again.
They tell her she was in a car accident.
I am brimming with confusion now.
They tell me she hit her head.
Again she asks what happened.
While the nurse tells her she was in a car
accident,
A doctor pulls me aside and tells me.
"Her blood alcohol level is almost double the
legal limit."
"That's all," he says.
I nod while inside I scream That's all???
That can't be all.
My confusion is palpable.

That's All

Mom's hospitalization lasts more days.
Fuzzy on details
Not to worry, they tell me.
She did hit her head after all.
That's all.
And her blood alcohol level was practically
twice the legal limit.
Of course she's confused.
Something else is wrong, I insist.
I can tell they humor me as they continue to
observe,
Watching and waiting.
It might be something else, they tell me
On day four when she asks again
Why am I in the hospital?

Condo Insanity

Stopping by the condo,
I am overwhelmed by its disarray
Wine bottles litter the counter and recycling bin
All of them empty
Empty, jumbo-sized bottles
Full ones in the refrigerator
Dirty socks and wadded up tissues are
everywhere
On the bedside table is a half-full wine glass and
a pill
Something is very wrong.
This is not my mother.

Hostility and the Quiz

Some random young lady comes in to ask Mom
questions
assessing her mental state.
Furious that it took four days before they would
even consider a different issue than liquor and a
head injury,
I stand with my arms crossed and lips pursed
Knowing mom will fail these questions.
Did she know the year?
No
Did she know the date?
No - even though it was written boldly on a
white board in her room
Did she know her own birthday?
No
Could she draw the face of a clock?
No
In the hall, the lady admitted that there were
some deficiencies.
She suggested the Neuro-psychologist on staff.
I suggested that when a family member tells one
of her team that there is an issue,
perhaps they may want to take that family
member seriously.
She nods.
And we have a six month wait to see the doctor.

Skip Denial, Go Straight to Anger

Surely we spent time in the land of Denial.
But we didn't realize.
Denial was the time Mom decided to drive to
Ohio for a funeral and got lost and panicked
calling my cousins to come and get her.
Denial was taking a family trip where we also
got totally lost and she didn't know what to do.
Denial was her waking up at 3:00 a.m., driving
to work, and sitting in the parking lot wondering
where everyone was.
Denial was her leaving groceries out to rot and
then trying to eat them anyway.
There was much denial, mainly her denial that
there was a problem.
Anger became my problem

September - The First Visit

Mom is hostile this time.
The kind doctor asks questions to get
background information.
Mom goes to another room to take a battery of
tests.
The kind doctor asks me questions about any
noticeable behaviors .
Mom takes a while to finish up.
The kind doctor scores the tests.
Mom is on the defensive.
The kind doctor agrees that there are
deficiencies.
But nothing too earth-shattering.
She suggests that Mom needs to give up the
alcohol.
Surprise - Mom already did. One month sober.
The kind doctor wants us to come back in June
to check for progression or possibly
improvement.
I'm hopeful but fresh out of optimism.

Covid

A student took an amazing tropical vacation and
came back at the end of February.
I took sick about that time as well.
Couldn't smell
Couldn't taste
Coughing, fever, congestion
I was on death's door.
There were no tests, but I knew based on the
symptoms and timing.
So, when the world was on lock down, I couldn't
help my mother, myself.
Confined to my bed in self-exile, I had groceries
delivered for us and for her.
My children helped with our deliveries.
Generous friends dropped off groceries or a
meal.
But who was helping Mom?

Busy Bee

While the lock down raged on,
Mom was busy.
Showing up for doctor and dentist appointments
All of which had been cancelled by the offices
Some office staff were quite unkind.
Mom kept busy
Inviting pushy salespeople into her condo
To sell her a $5,000 custom-made sliding glass
door.
Later she forgot she purchased the door.
Mom stayed busy
Ordering another door at a big box retailer.
They, too, entered her condo during lock down
to measure.
Stupid doors made of glass are easy to shatter.
As the lock down continued.

June - The Second Visit

I dreaded that second visit to the
Neuro-psychologist.
Knowing there was no improvement, expecting
bad news,
Waiting while tests were administered again.
It took much longer for this go-around.
"We think it's Vascular Dementia," she said.
Nails pounding into the coffin of my broken
heart.
"She doesn't have any other heath factors, and
she's young."
Furiously, Mom sat in her chair, arms crossed,
almost folding in on herself.
Scans and tests were run, but it was still
Vascular Dementia.
I started handling the bills.
Mom retired.
My "Constant Worry" era began.

October - The Car

It was a random day when Cousin Nick called.
Apologizing at length before explaining what
happened.
Mom stopped at his car dealership.
She was lost and confused.
On her way to a doctor's appointment, she forgot
the way.
Recognizing the dealership, she pulled in for
help.
Cousin Nick helped her call the doctor.
But her appointment was for another few weeks.
For safety purposes, I took the car keys.

December

December came.
Her days and nights
were mixed up.
She was wandering
out of her condo,
locking herself out.
We needed a change.
Home health seemed like
A viable option.
What came next was
a long line of
in-home companions.
Some were fantastic,
and Mom enjoyed them.
A couple were
disappointments,
and Mom did not enjoy
that.

A Year Later

It was time for round-the-clock care.
We found a nice place.
Mom picked out furniture.
And it was as homey
as we could make it.
With pictures and books
and nice, new towels.
But it wasn't home.

Two Years Later

Two years later,
Mom is not herself.
She wanders, safely,
in her two year old home.
Needing help with most basic tasks,
with a high standard of care.
Guilt and sadness are overwhelming.
Obsessing over decisions I made.
Afraid they weren't the best.
Do I visit enough?
Does she know she is loved?
Could I have been more patient?
All the while, these questions turn
over in my head, I plan.
Plan so her grandchildren
won't have to do for me
what I've done for her.
Not because I resent it.
But because I don't want
them to go through it.
No child should have to watch
their parent slowly lose every part
that made them whole.
So mine won't.
That alone gives me peace.

Mornings

Mornings don't bother me like some.
But leaving the warmth of the bed is a struggle.
Mornings mean rushing, feeding dogs, enduring
the revolving door of in and out - out and in.
Mornings are a quick prep of myself and
lunch for work if I have the time.
Mornings are making sure the kid is
awake and readying himself for the day.
Mornings are school drop-offs and
finding a decent parking spot for myself.
But sometimes...
Mornings are pauses at a stoplight
or the parking lot.
Pauses to stop and stare at a magnificent, fiery
sunrise
with bright, pink, cotton-candy clouds painting
the sky
like symmetrical bouncy houses all in a row.
Those mornings make everything worthwhile.

Loki

The boys wanted a dog, and so did I.
We found an owner with an unexpected litter of
pups.
There were five, but one had problem paws in
front.
"He's special," my oldest said, wiser at 10 than
most 20 year olds.
"We are special, so he should be with us," he
said, and
his little brother agreed.
Our family dog was chosen.
He was shy at first and slept a lot,
snuggly and warm with a new-puppy-coffee
smell.
Soon he grew and found the most wondrous
toys.
(Mostly he played with Mom's leather shoes.)
The boys named him Loki.
A fitting name for a Dog of Mischief

Another Fluffy Monster

One day post-Covid, immersed by Mom's issues,
I decided we needed more joy in our lives.
A friend had just gotten an adorable Labrador.
"There's one left in the litter," my friend told me.
Sold.
I met the breeder, the puppy, and the puppy's
dog parents
on a weekend when the kids were not with me.
This puppy had an overbite, and no one wanted
him either.
We were given this sweet pup at no cost.
A loving home was all that was required.
"He will be loved with us," I assured.
After all, he was a rescue of sorts.
Should've done my homework.
Labradors are high energy, but this one was off
the charts.
Counter-surfing and trash-eating
were his pastimes.
Eating socks and chewing up clothes
were his hobbies.
Dumping his water and food bowls
were his dining rituals.
Despite all that, he is fun-loving and
affectionate.

Always happy to see us and crumbs on the floor.
And he follows me everywhere...
even to the bathroom!
My sweet Falcon.

Second Chances

When you get a second chance, you have to take it.
Be brave.
Try new foods.
Experience new cultures.
Love yourself, all of yourself, completely.
Engage in new hobbies.
Meet new people.
Go all in with everything you have.
And when you get a second chance at love.
Break down that door.
Feel it.
Even if you are afraid.
You are worth it, worth being loved.
When you get a second chance, you have to take it.